Love

Gabriella

ARIEL BOOKS

**Andrews McMeel
Publishing**

Kansas City

Abounding Happiness

A TREASURY OF WISDOM

EDITED, WITH COMMENTARY, BY

M. Scott Peck, M.D.

AUTHOR OF THE ROAD LESS TRAVELED

03   04   05   06   07   KWF   10   9   8   7   6   5   4   3   2   1

ISBN: 0-7407-3335-4

Library of Congress Catalog Card Number: 2002111564

contents

PREFACE 7

INTRODUCTION 9

ACCEPTANCE 17

CHEERFULNESS 32

CONTENTMENT 41

FORGIVENESS 55

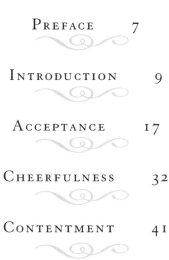

GRATITUDE   66

HUMOR   74

SERENITY   82

HAPPINESS   88

EPILOGUE   126

preface

In 2000, M. Scott Peck edited a collection of his favorite quotations in a beautiful volume called *Abounding Grace: An Anthology of Wisdom.* These words, gleaned from writers and thinkers, both famous and obscure, ancient and modern, were chosen to serve as guideposts on the road to a more spiritual existence.

Abounding Happiness is developed from one of the twelve sections of *Abounding Grace.* The book not only includes all the quotations from the Happiness section of *Abounding Grace* and Dr. Peck's introductory commentary, but a number of new quotations as well.

introduction

$\mathcal{U}$NQUESTIONABLY, IT IS human nature to desire happiness, at any time and at any place.

This desire, this inherent part of us, may also be the root of what Christian theologians call original sin. Why else would Adam and Eve have disobeyed God by eating the forbidden fruit of the Tree of the Knowledge of Good and Evil unless they thought they might somehow become even happier as a result?

I am often asked why I began my first book with the sentence: "Life is difficult." My answer is always, "Because I wanted to combat the Lie."

The Lie is that we are here on earth to be comfortable, happy, and fulfilled. Is that not our very purpose for being? Certainly it is the message with which we are bombarded by the media every possible minute, catering to our original sin by suggesting that if we're not feeling comfortable, happy, or fulfilled, then something must be terribly wrong: We must not own the right car; we must not be eating the right cereal; or worst of all, we must not have it right with God.

The truth is that our finest moments are most likely to occur when we are feeling deeply uncomfortable, unhappy, or unfulfilled. For it is only in such moments, propelled by our discomfort, that we are likely to step out of our ruts and start searching for different ways or truer answers—or even for God.

William James defined generic religion (or spirituality, if you will) as "the attempt to be in harmony with an unseen order of things." Among the quotes that follow, Henry Miller (an author more renowned for sexuality than spirituality) strangely echoes James when he says: "The world is not to be put in order; the world is in order. It is for us to put ourselves in unison with this order."

Although both Miller and James imply that being in harmony with this invisible order is a secret— perhaps *the* secret—to happiness, neither of them intended it to sound like a simple matter. The order is, after all, invisible and hence inevitably mysterious, as well as beyond manipulation. It is often not what we think it is and certainly often not what we want it to be. Yet it does give us hints of itself, revelations, although not necessarily according to our schedule. It (God, to me) even occasionally speaks to us through that "still, small voice." And one of the things I myself have heard it say repeatedly is: "There's more to life than happiness."

For example, one of the components of happiness, listed here as a virtue in its own right, is contentment. Fine, but does God or the unseen order want us to be content with murder? With rape? With slavery? With a caste system or any other systematic form of oppression? No! And so, paradoxically, there is something we have come to correctly call "divine discontent."

Ah, paradox, as always. There are at least two sides to everything. Having decried the desire for happiness as the possible root of original sin, let me now extol it as the possible root of "original virtue." Was it a bad thing that Adam and Eve developed the knowledge of good and evil and were cast out of the womb of Eden? In the long run, I think not.

I proclaimed that our finest moments more often than not are occasions of profound unhappiness, of "divine discontent." Why is this so? It is because our desire for happiness propels us in situations of unhappiness to rectify the situation. Sometimes our attempts at rectification are bumbling, even fatal. Drug abuse or suicide are examples. At other times, however, our attempts at rectification are noble. The result may be repentance or conversion to a more spiritual life—or some other form of personal healing and *change*. Possibly even grand social change. Whether its cause was the unhappiness of simple fatigue or of victimization I do not know, but I do know it was divine discontent that gave Rosa Parks the courage to refuse to move to the back of the bus that afternoon in December 1955.

So, by all means, seek happiness. But do so wisely. Conflicting though they may sometimes seem, the quotes that follow offer many clues for success in finding the necessary wisdom.

The idea that happiness as an unmodified goal will likely be self-defeating keeps popping up. Seek to be loved and you probably won't be; seek to love, on the other hand, and you probably will be. Look solely for happiness, and I doubt you'll find it. Forget about happiness, seek wisdom and goodness, and probably happiness will find you. Happiness is usually indirect, a side effect or by-product of something else.

What "something else"? No one thing. The component virtues that follow—acceptance, cheerfulness, contentment, forgiveness, humor, serenity, and, above all, gratitude—are all such other things, and therefore clues. You cannot be fully happy, for instance, if there is someone in your life you currently hate. Yet there are twists and turns. Some of the quotes acknowledge the reality that it is necessary to judge a man guilty of a crime before it is possible to genuinely pardon him. All else is what I have labeled "cheap forgiveness." Forgiveness is the relinquishment of anger. There can be no real forgiveness without there first being real and righteous anger. If not held onto for too long, righteous "holy" anger is one of the most God-given of emotions.

Finally, it seems to me that the virtues must work hand in hand, sometimes smoothly "in synch" and sometimes out of the conflicting turmoil of agonizing over what is right and what is wrong, each in its own place and time.

In this book there is a focus upon acceptance and serenity. These virtues, along with others such as courage and wisdom, are all necessary ingredients of the same stew. Nowhere is this more clear than in the famed Serenity Prayer, popularized by the Twelve-

Step Program but attributed to the theologian, Reinhold Niebuhr:

O God, grant me the serenity

To accept the things I cannot change,

The courage to change the things I can,

And the wisdom to know the difference.

acceptance

I accept the universe!
— MARGARET FULLER

*T*here are people who live lives little different
   than the beasts, and I don't mean that badly.
   I mean that they accept whatever happens day
   to day without struggle or question or regret.
   To them things just are, like the earth and sky
   and seasons.
— CELESTE DE BLASIS

*E*verything in life that we really accept undergoes a change.

—KATHERINE MANSFIELD

*W*hen we have accepted the worst, we have nothing more to lose. And that automatically means—we have everything to gain.

—DALE CARNEGIE

*I*f a man does not keep pace with his companions, perhaps it is because he hears a different drummer. Let him step to the music which he hears, however measured or far away.

—HENRY DAVID THOREAU

*G*od does not make clones. Each person is different, a tribute to God's creativity. If we are to
love our neighbors as ourselves, we must accept
people as they are and not demand that they
conform to our own image.

—HENRY FEHREN

*I*t just ain't possible to explain some things. It's
interesting to wonder on them and do some
speculation, but the main thing is you have to
accept it—take it for what it is, and get on with
your growing.

—JIM DODGE

*Y*ou must shift your sail with the wind.
———ITALIAN PROVERB

*G*rowth begins when we start to accept our own
weakness.
———JEAN VANIER

I didn't belong as a kid, and that always bothered
me. If only I'd known that one day my differ-
entness would be an asset, then my early life
would have been much easier.
———BETTE MIDLER

Learn not to sweat the small stuff.

—DR. KENNETH GREENSPAN

If you can alter things, alter them. If you cannot, put up with them.

—ENGLISH PROVERB

Do you know why that cow looks over that wall? . . . She looks over the wall because she cannot see through it, and that is what you must do with your troubles—look over and *above* them.

—JOHN WESLEY

*W*e all may have come on different ships, but we're in the same boat now.

—MARTIN LUTHER KING JR.

*A*cceptance is not submission; it is acknowledgment of the facts of a situation. Then deciding what you're going to do about it.

—KATHLEEN CASEY THEISEN

*Y*ou have to take it as it happens, but you should try to make it happen the way you want to take it.

—GERMAN PROVERB

First ask yourself: What is the worst that can
    happen? Then prepare to accept it. Then
    proceed to improve on the worst.
                    —DALE CARNEGIE

God asks no man whether he will accept life.
    This is not the choice. You must take it.
    The only question is how.
                    —HENRY WARD BEECHER

To repel one's cross is to make it heavier.
                    —HENRI FRÉDÉRIC AMIEL

*T*here are two ways of meeting difficulties: you
alter the difficulties, or you alter yourself to
meet them.
—PHYLLIS BOTTOME

*A*nything in life that we don't accept will
simply make trouble for us until we make
peace with it.
—SHAKTI GAWAIN

*L*ife is not always what one wants it to be, but to
make the best of it, as it is, is the only way of
being happy.
—JENNIE JEROME CHURCHILL

True freedom lies in the realization and calm
acceptance of the fact that there may very
well be no perfect answer.
—ALLEN REID MCGINNIS

Arrange whatever pieces come your way.
—VIRGINIA WOOLF

I have accepted fear as a part of life—specifically
the fear of change. . . . I have gone ahead
despite the pounding in the heart that says:
turn back.
—ERICA JONG

You are responsible for your life. You can't keep blaming somebody else for your dysfunction. . . . Life is really about moving on.

— OPRAH WINFREY

Argue for your limitations, and sure enough, they're yours.

— RICHARD BACH

Life is not so much a problem to be solved as a mystery to be lived.

— ANONYMOUS

My advice to you is not to inquire why or whither, but just enjoy your ice cream while it's on your plate.

—THORNTON WILDER

Ah, when to the heart of a man
Was it ever less than a treason
To go with the drift of things,
To yield with a grace to reason,
And bow and accept the end
Of a love or a season?

—ROBERT FROST

*A*ccept things as they are, not as you wish them to be.
— NAPOLEON I

A man is rich in proportion to the number of things which he can afford to let alone.
— HENRY DAVID THOREAU

*B*e willing to have it so; acceptance of what has happened is the first step to overcoming the consequences of any misfortune.
— WILLIAM JAMES

*W*hy not be oneself? That is the whole secret of a successful appearance. If one is a greyhound, why try to look like a Pekingese?

—DAME EDITH SITWELL

*W*e know nothing of tomorrow; our business is to be good and happy today.

—SYDNEY SMITH

I have a simple philosophy. Fill what's empty. Empty what's full. And scratch where it itches.

—ALICE ROOSEVELT LONGWORTH

Are we to look at cherry blossoms only in full bloom, the moon only when it is cloudless? To long for the moon while looking on the rain, to lower the blinds and be unaware of the passing of the spring—these are even more deeply moving. Branches about to blossom or gardens strewn with flowers are worthier of our admiration.

—YOSHIDA KENKO

The man who has lived the longest is not he who has spent the greatest number of years, but he who has had the greatest sensibility of life.

—JEAN-JACQUES ROUSSEAU

The art of life lies in a constant readjustment to
our surroundings.
—OKAKURA KAKUZO

Acceptance is the activity of love.
—SAMUEL KIRSHMER

Always fall in love with what you're asked to
accept. Take what is given, and make it over
your way. My aim in life has always been to
hold my own with whatever's going. Not
against: with.
—ROBERT FROST

cheerfulness

I have always preferred cheerfulness to mirth.
  The latter I consider as an act, the former as
  an habit of mind. Mirth is short and transient,
  cheerfulness fixed and permanent.
  —JOSEPH ADDISON

*K*eep a green tree in your heart and perhaps the
  singing bird will come.
  —CHINESE PROVERB

A good-natured man has the whole world to be
happy out of.
— ALEXANDER POPE

*F*ew are qualified to shine in company, but it is in
most men's power to be agreeable.
— JONATHAN SWIFT

I felt an earnest and humble desire, and shall do
till I die, to increase the stock of harmless
cheerfulness.
— CHARLES DICKENS

There is nothing more beautiful than cheerfulness
in an old face.
—JEAN PAUL RICHTER

A happy woman is one who has no cares at all;
a cheerful woman is one who has cares but
doesn't let them get her down.
—BEVERLY SILLS

Cheerfulness, it would appear, is a matter which
depends fully as much on the state of things
within, as on the state of things without and
around us.
—CHARLOTTE BRONTË

A cheerful temper, joined with innocence will
make beauty attractive, knowledge delightful,
and wit good-natured.
— JOSEPH ADDISON

I am still determined to be cheerful and happy in
whatever situation I may be, for I have also
learned from experience that the greater part
of our happiness or misery depends on our dis-
positions and not on our circumstances.
— MARTHA WASHINGTON

T he best part of health is fine disposition.
— RALPH WALDO EMERSON

The best way to cheer yourself up is to try to cheer somebody else up.

—MARK TWAIN

The teeth are smiling, but is the heart?

—CONGOLESE PROVERB

Cheerfulness is contagious, but don't wait to catch it from others. Be a carrier!

—ANONYMOUS

Be of good cheer: this counsel is of Heaven.

—HOMER

*G*ood nature is worth more than knowledge,
more than money, more than honor, to the
persons who possess it.

———Henry Ward Beecher

*G*ood-humor is a philosophic state of mind; it
seems to say to Nature that we take her no
more seriously than she takes us.

———Ernest Renan

*C*heerfulness keeps up a kind of daylight in the
mind, and fills it with a steady and perpetual
serenity.

———Joseph Addison

*W*hile there is a chance of the world getting through its troubles, I hold that a reasonable man has to behave as though he were sure of it. If at the end your cheerfulness is not justified, at any rate you will have been cheerful.

—H. G. WELLS

*O*f cheerfulness, or a good temper—the more it is spent, the more of it remains.

—RALPH WALDO EMERSON

*C*heerfulness, in most cheerful people, is the rich and satisfying result of strenuous discipline.

—EDWIN PERCY WHIPPLE

A merry heart maketh a cheerful countenance.
—Proverb

*T*he plainest sign of wisdom is a continual cheerfulness: her state is like that of things in the
regions above the moon, always clear and
serene.
—Michel de Montaigne

*W*ondrous is the strength of cheerfulness, and its
power of endurance—the cheerful man will do
more in the same time, will do it better, will
preserve it longer, than the sad or sullen.
—Thomas Carlyle

$\mathcal{F}$ake feeling good. You may have the most legitimate reason in the world to be unhappy. You may have lost someone important to you, you may have lost your job, you may be a stranger in town, you may be recovering from a broken romance. But when you're with people, don't wear your depression like a badge. You're going to have to learn to fake cheerfulness. Believe it or not, eventually that effort will pay off: you'll actually start feeling happier.

———JEAN BACH

$\mathcal{T}$he true source of cheerfulness is benevolence.

———P. GODWIN

contentment

*B*e content with your lot; one cannot be first in
everything.
— AESOP

*C*ontent may dwell in all stations. To be low,
but above contempt, may be high enough to
be happy.
— SIR THOMAS BROWNE

*B*etter a little fire to warm us than a great one to
burn us.
— THOMAS FULLER, M.D.

*H*e may well be contented who needs neither
borrow nor flatter.
— JOHN RAY

*O*h, don't the days seem lank and long,
When all goes right and nothing goes wrong
And isn't your life extremely flat
With nothing whatever to grumble at!
— W. S. GILBERT

*N*othing will content him who is not content
with a little.

—GREEK PROVERB

*A*ll fortune belongs to him who has a contented
mind. Is not the whole earth covered with
leather for him whose feet are encased in
shoes?

—PANCHATANTRA

*I*f thou covetest riches, ask not but for contentment, which is an immense treasure.

—SA'DI

*G*ood friends, good books, and a sleepy conscience: this is the ideal life.
—MARK TWAIN

*M*y crown is in my heart, not on my head;
Not deck'd with diamonds and Indian stones,
Nor to be seen: my crown is called content;
A crown it is that seldom kings enjoy.
—WILLIAM SHAKESPEARE

*W*hen we cannot find contentment in ourselves it
is useless to seek it elsewhere.
—LA ROCHEFOUCAULD

*F*at hens lay few eggs.

—GERMAN PROVERB

*H*appy the man, of mortals happiest he,
Whose quiet mind from vain desires is free;
Whom neither hopes deceive, nor fears torment,
But lives at peace, within himself content.

—GEORGE GRANVILLE

*T*he utmost we can hope for in this world is
contentment; if we aim at anything higher,
we shall meet with nothing but grief and
disappointment.

—JOSEPH ADDISON

[45]

Content makes poor men rich; discontent makes rich men poor.

—Benjamin Franklin

The secret of contentment is the realization that life is a gift, not a right.

—Anonymous

Do not spoil what you have by desiring what you have not; but remember that what you now have was once among the things only hoped for.

—Epicurus

Notwithstanding the poverty of my outside experience, I have always had a significance for myself, and every chance to stumble along my straight and narrow little path, and to worship at the feet of my Deity, and what more can a human soul ask for?

—ALICE JAMES

You can't have everything. Where would you put it?

—STEVEN WRIGHT

Who is content with nothing possesses all things.

—NICHOLAS BOILEAU

There are nine requisites for contented living:
health enough to make work a pleasure; wealth
enough to support your needs; strength to battle
with difficulties and overcome them; grace
enough to confess your sins and forsake them;
patience enough to toil until some good is
accomplished; charity enough to see some good
in your neighbor; love enough to move you to
be useful and helpful to others; faith enough to
make real the things of God; hope enough to
remove all anxious fears concerning the future.
—JOHANN WOLFGANG VON GOETHE

I am easily satisfied with the very best.
—WINSTON CHURCHILL

I have learned, in whatsoever state I am, therewith to be content.

—PHILIPPIANS 4:11

For me, there was always a sense of contentment in feeling a rhythm beneath my feet. The heartbeat of the land. That season would follow season and that the rhythm would never alter. Knowing this brought me peace like no other I had known.

—WITI IHIMAERA

Well-being is attained by little and little, and nevertheless it is no little thing itself.

—ZENO OF CITIUM

*P*eople are always good company when they are doing what they really enjoy.
—SAMUEL BUTLER

I would do what I pleased, and doing what I pleased, I should have my will, and having my will, I should be contented; and when one is contented, there is no more to be desired; and when there is no more to be desired, there is an end of it.
—CERVANTES

*H*e who is contented is rich.
—LAO-TSU

'Tis better to be lowly born,
And range with humble livers in content,
Than to be perk'd up in a glistering grief,
And wear a golden sorrow.
—WILLIAM SHAKESPEARE

Fit thyself into the environment that thou findest
    on earth, and love the men with whom thy lot
    is cast.
—MARCUS AURELIUS

I have guarded myself more carefully against con-
    tented people than against contagious diseases.
—VICTORIE WOLFF

No one is contented in this world, I believe.
There is always something left to desire, and
the last thing longed for always seems the most
necessary to happiness.
———MARIE CORELLI

It's not a very big step from contentment to
complacency.
———SIMONE DE BEAUVOIR

Contentment is a pearl of great price, and whoever
procures it at the expense of ten thousand
desires makes a wise and happy purchase.
———JOHN BALGUY

Like a cat asleep in a chair
At peace, in peace
And at one with the master of the house,
with the mistress,
At home, at home in the house of the living,
Sleeping on the hearth, and yawning
before the fire.

—D. H. LAWRENCE

It is right to be contented with what we have, but
never with what we are.

—SIR JAMES MACKINTOSH

*T*here is no paycheck that can equal the feeling of
  contentment that comes from being the person
  you are meant to be.
  —OPRAH WINFREY

*W*e may pass violets looking for roses. We may
  pass contentment looking for victory.
  —BERN WILLIAMS

forgiveness

To err is human, to forgive, divine.
———Alexander Pope

Forgiving presupposes remembering.
———Paul Tillich

Once a woman has forgiven her man, she must
not reheat his sins for breakfast.
———Marlene Dietrich

The truest joys they seldom prove,
    Who free from quarrels live;
'Tis the most tender part of love,
    Each other to forgive.
        —JOHN SHEFFIELD

A wise man will make haste to forgive, because
he knows the true value of time, and will not
suffer it to pass away in unnecessary pain.
        —SAMUEL JOHNSON

Forgive others often, but yourself never.
        —LATIN PROVERB

In taking revenge a man is but even with his
enemy, but in passing it over he is superior,
for it is a prince's part to pardon.
—FRANCIS BACON

The stupid neither forgive nor forget;
The naive forgive and forget;
The wise forgive but do not forget.
—THOMAS SZASZ

If you haven't forgiven yourself something, how
can you forgive others?
—DOLORES HUERTA

*I*f you understand something, you don't forgive it,
 you are the thing itself: forgiveness is for what
 you *don't* understand.
 —DORIS LESSING

I think one should forgive and remember. . . . If
 you forgive and forget in the usual sense,
 you're just driving what you remember into
 the subconscious; it stays there and festers. But
 to look, even regularly, upon what you remember and *know* you've forgiven is achievement.
 —FAITH BALDWIN

The weak can never forgive. Forgiveness is the
attribute of the strong.
— MAHATMA GANDHI

Always forgive your enemies; nothing annoys
them so much.
— OSCAR WILDE

Children begin by loving their parents; as they
grow older they judge them; sometimes they
forgive them.
— OSCAR WILDE

*W*e must develop and maintain the capacity to forgive. He who is devoid of the power to forgive is devoid of the power to love. There is some good in the worst of us and some evil in the best of us. When we discover this, we are less prone to hate our enemies.

—MARTIN LUTHER KING JR.

*F*orgiveness is the key to action and freedom.

—HANNAH ARENDT

*F*or my part, I believe in the forgiveness of sin and the redemption of ignorance.

—ADLAI STEVENSON

*H*e that cannot forgive others breaks the bridge over which he must pass himself; for every man has need to be forgiven.

—THOMAS FULLER, M.D.

*D*on't carry a grudge. While you're carrying the grudge the other guy's out dancing.

—BUDDY HACKETT

*F*orgiveness is the fragrance the violet sheds on the heel that has crushed it.

—ANONYMOUS

*F*orgiveness is the act of admitting we are like other people.
— CHRISTINA BALDWIN

*A*fter a good dinner, one can forgive anybody, even one's own relatives.
— OSCAR WILDE

*F*orgive, son; men are men, they needs must err.
— EURIPIDES

I can pardon everyone's mistakes but my own.
— MARCUS PORCIUS CATO

*W*ithout forgiveness life is governed by . . . an endless cycle of resentment and retaliation.
—ROBERTO ASSAGIOLI

*N*ever does the human soul appear so strong as when it forgoes revenge, and dares forgive an injury.
—E. H. CHAPIN

*F*orgiveness is not an occasional act—it's a permanent attitude.
—MARTIN LUTHER KING JR.

*F*orgiveness is the economy of the heart. . . .
Forgiveness saves the expense of anger, the
cost of hatred, the waste of spirits.
———HANNAH MOORE

*A*s long as you don't forgive, who and whatever
it is will occupy rent-free space in your mind.
———ISABELLE HOLLAND

*W*e can forgive anything as long as it isn't done
to us.
———P. D. JAMES

It is very easy to forgive others their mistakes; it takes more grit and gumption to forgive them for having witnessed your own.

—Jessamyn West

You could have forgiven my committing a sin if you hadn't feared that I had committed a pleasure as well.

—Ellen Glasgow

Fear less; hope more. Eat less; chew more. Talk less; say more. Hate less; love more. And never underestimate the power of forgiveness.

—Abigail Van Buren

gratitude

*S*ome people are always grumbling because
roses have thorns; I am thankful that thorns
have roses.
— ALPHONSE KARR

*T*he sign outside the gates of salvation says,
"Be grateful."
— MICHAEL LEVINE

*E*very time I fill a vacant office, I make ten
malcontents and one ingrate.

— Louis XIV

*I*nto the well which supplies thee with water,
cast no stones.

— Talmud

*I*t is a dangerous thing to ask why someone else
has been given more. It is humbling—and
indeed healthy—to ask why you have been
given so much.

— Condoleezza Rice

*L*et us give thanks for this beautiful day. Let us give thanks for this life. Let us give thanks for the water without which life would not be possible. Let us give thanks for Grandmother Earth who protects and nourishes us.

—DAILY PRAYER OF THE
LAKOTA AMERICAN INDIAN

*W*hen eating bamboo sprouts, remember the man who planted them.

—CHINESE PROVERB

A thankful heart is the parent of all virtues.

—CICERO

*L*et me say that the credit belongs to the boys in the back rooms. It isn't the man who sits in the limelight like me who should have the praise. It is not the men who sit in prominent places. It is the men in the back rooms.

—LORD BEAVERBROOK

*W*ise men appreciate all men, for they see the good in each and know how hard it is to make anything good.

—BALTASAR GRACIÁN

*G*ratitude is the heart's memory.

—FRENCH PROVERB

I would rather be able to appreciate things I can not have than to have things I am not able to appreciate.

—ELBERT HUBBARD

*N*o duty is more urgent than that of returning thanks.

—SAINT AMBROSE

*I*f a fellow isn't thankful for what he's got, he isn't likely to be thankful for what he's going to get.

—FRANK A. CLARK

*H*e who returns favors is remembered
afterwards, and when he totters, he will
find support.
— BEN SIRA

*D*on't drown the man who taught you to swim.
— ENGLISH PROVERB

*G*ive a grateful man more than he asks.
— PORTUGUESE PROVERB

*W*hen befriended, remember it. When you befriend, forget it.
— BENJAMIN FRANKLIN

I would maintain that thanks are the highest form of thought; and that gratitude is happiness doubled by wonder.
— G. K. CHESTERTON

O thou who has given us so much, mercifully grant us one thing more—a grateful heart.
— GEORGE HERBERT

Sweet is the breath of vernal shower,
The bee's collected treasures sweet,
Sweet music's melting fall, but sweeter yet
The still small voice of gratitude.
———Thomas Gray

One of life's gifts is that each of us, no
matter how downtrodden, finds reasons
for thankfulness.
———J. Robert Meskin

Humor

*M*en will let you abuse them if only you will make them laugh.
— HENRY WARD BEECHER

A sense of humor keen enough to show a man his own absurdities, as well as those of other people, will keep him from the commission of all sins, or nearly all, save those that are worth committing.
— SAMUEL BUTLER

As brevity is the soul of wit, form, it seems to me, is the heart of humor and the salvation of comedy.

— JAMES THURBER

Men will confess to treason, murder, arson, false teeth, or a wig. How many of them will own up to a lack of humor?

— FRANK MOORE COLBY

A difference of taste in jokes is a great strain on the affections.

— GEORGE ELIOT

*H*umor simultaneously wounds and heals, indicts and pardons, diminishes and enlarges; it constitutes inner growth at the expense of outer gain, and those who possess and honestly practice it make themselves more through a willingness to make themselves less.

—LOUIS KRONENBERGER

*I*t's hard to be funny when you have to be clean.

—MAE WEST

*W*it has truth in it; wisecracking is simply calisthenics with words.

—DOROTHY PARKER

Closely related to faith; [humor] bids us not to take
anything too seriously.
—FULTON J. SHEEN

The humorist has a good eye for the humbug; he
does not always recognize the saint.
—W. SOMERSET MAUGHAM

Humor is a serious thing. I like to think of it
as one of our greatest and earliest national
resources which must be preserved at all costs.
—JAMES THURBER

*H*umour is by far the most significant activity of the human brain.
—EDWARD DE BONO

*H*umor is the shortest distance between two people.
—VICTOR BORGE

*H*umor is an affirmation of dignity, a declaration of man's superiority to all that befalls him.
—ROMAIN GARY

A jest often decides matters of importance more effectually and happily than seriousness.
—HORACE

E verything is funny as long as it is happening to somebody else.
—WILL ROGERS

F un is a good thing but only when it spoils nothing better.
—GEORGE SANTAYANA

*H*umor is laughing at what you haven't got
when you ought to have it.
— LANGSTON HUGHES

*H*e deserves paradise who makes his companions laugh.
— QUR'AN

*A*mong those whom I like or admire, I can find
no common denominator, but among those
whom I love, I can: All of them can make me
laugh.
— W. H. AUDEN

*W*it is a weapon. Jokes are a masculine way
of inflicting superiority. But humour is the
pursuit of a gentle grin, usually in solitude.
———FRANK MUIR

*D*rama and humor come from trouble and
sadness, and mankind's astounding ability
to survive life's unhappiness.
———CHARLES SCHULZ

serenity

There is no joy but calm.

— ALFRED, LORD TENNYSON

Do not let trifles disturb your tranquility of
mind. . . . Life is too precious to be sacrificed
for the nonessential and transient. . . . Ignore
the inconsequential.

— GRENVILLE KLEISER

*A*s a rule, for no one does life drag more dis-
agreeably than for him who tries to speed it up.
— JEAN PAUL RICHTER

I have laid aside business, and gone a-fishing.
— IZAAK WALTON

*D*o not seek to have everything that happens
happen as you wish, but wish for everything to
happen as it actually does happen, and your life
will be serene.
— EPICTETUS

The world is not to be put in order, the world is in
order. It is for us to put ourselves in unison
with this order.
—HENRY MILLER

Were all the year one constant sunshine, we
Should have no flowers,
All would be draught and leanness; not a tree
Would make us bowers;
Beauty consists in colors; and that's best
Which is not fixed, but flies and flowers.
—HENRY VAUGHAN

In the depth of winter, I finally learned that within me there lay an invincible summer.

—ALBERT CAMUS

Serenity comes not alone by removing the outward causes and occasions of fear, but by the discovery of inward reservoirs to draw upon.

—RUFUS M. JONES

Do not be in a hurry to fill up an empty space with words and embellishments, before it has been filled with a deep interior peace.

—ALEXANDER ELCHANINOV

*I*f you want inner peace find it in solitude, not
speed, and if you would find yourself, look to
the land from which you came and to which
you go.
—STEWART L. UDALL

*B*ack of tranquility lies always
conquered unhappiness.
—DAVID GRAYSON

*L*earn the sweet magic of a cheerful face;
Not always smiling, but at least serene.
—OLIVER WENDELL HOLMES

*D*eep within us all there is an amazing inner
sanctuary of the soul, a holy place, a Divine
Center, a speaking Voice. . . . Life from the
Center is a life of unhurried peace and power.
It is simple. It is serene. It is amazing. It is
radiant.
—T. R. KELLY

*N*othing can bring you peace but yourself.
—RALPH WALDO EMERSON

*Y*ou must learn to be still in the midst of activity
and to be vibrantly alive in repose.
—INDIRA GANDHI

Happiness

*H*appiness depends upon ourselves.
—Aristotle

*T*he bird of paradise alights only upon the hand
that does not grasp.
—John Berry

*H*e that is of a merry heart hath a continual
feast.
—Proverbs 15:15

*O*ne moment may with bliss repay
Unnumbered hours of pain.
—Thomas Campbell

*T*o be happy, we must not be too concerned with
others.
—Albert Camus

*H*appiness, that grand mistress of the
ceremonies in the dance of life, impels us
through all its mazes and meanderings,
but leads none of us by the same route.
——CHARLES CALEB COLTON

*T*rue joy is the nearest which we have of heaven,
it is the treasure of the soul, and therefore
should be laid in a safe place, and nothing in
this world is safe to place it in.
——JOHN DONNE

*H*uman felicity is produced not so much by great pieces of good fortune that seldom happen as by little advantages that occur every day.

——Benjamin Franklin

*H*appiness makes up in height for what it lacks in length.

——Robert Frost

*W*hen one door of happiness closes, another opens; but often we look so long at the closed door that we do not see the one which has been opened for us.

——Helen Keller

*H*appiness is itself a kind of gratitude.
—JOSEPH WOOD KRUTCH

*W*hen you jump for joy, beware that no one
moves the ground from beneath your feet.
—STANISLAW LEC

I am happy and content because I think I am.
—ALAIN-RÉNÉ LESAGE

*T*here are many roads
to happiness, if the gods assent.
—PINDAR

*N*o man is happy who does not think himself so.
—PUBLILIUS SYRUS

*M*an needs, for his happiness, not only the
enjoyment of this or that, but hope and
enterprise and change.
—BERTRAND RUSSELL

I find my joy of living in the fierce and ruthless
battles of life, and my pleasure comes from
learning something.
—AUGUST STRINDBERG

The trouble is not that we are never happy—it is that happiness is so episodical.

—RUTH BENEDICT

Happiness? A good cigar, a good meal, a good cigar and a good woman—or a bad woman; it depends on how much happiness you can handle.

—GEORGE BURNS

That is happiness; to be dissolved into something complete and great.

—WILLA CATHER

*P*eople need joy quite as much as clothing. Some of them need it far more.

—Margaret Collier Graham

*H*appiness is a habit—cultivate it.

—Elbert Hubbard

*H*ow to gain, how to keep, how to recover happiness is in fact for most men at all times the secret motive of all they do, and of all they are willing to endure.

—William James

*K*issing your hand may make you feel very, very good but a diamond and sapphire bracelet lasts forever.

———Anita Loos

*P*uritanism—the haunting fear that someone, somewhere, may be happy.

———H. L. Mencken

*W*here's the man could ease a heart
Like a satin gown?

———Dorothy Parker

*H*appiness is a way-station between too little and
too much.
— CHANNING POLLOCK

*M*odern Americans travel light, with little
philosophic baggage other than a fervent belief
in their right to the pursuit of happiness.
— GEORGE WILL

*M*y life has no purpose, no direction, no aim,
no meaning, and yet I'm happy. I can't figure it
out. What am I doing right?
— CHARLES SCHULZ

The secret of happiness is this: Let your interests be as wide as possible, and let your reactions to the things and persons that interest you be as far as possible friendly rather than hostile.
—BERTRAND RUSSELL

The happy man is not he who seems thus to others, but who seems thus to himself.
—PUBLILIUS SYRUS

There is nothing which has yet been contrived by man by which so much happiness is produced as by a good tavern.
—SAMUEL JOHNSON

If happiness truly consisted in physical ease and freedom from care, then the happiest individual would not be either a man or a woman; it would be, I think, an American cow.
——WILLIAM LYON PHELPS

The happiest man is he who learns from nature the lesson of worship.
——RALPH WALDO EMERSON

If you ever find happiness by hunting for it, you will find it, as the old woman did her lost spectacles, safe on her own nose all the time.
——JOSH BILLINGS

*I*f a man has important work, and enough leisure and income to enable him to do it properly, he is in possession of as much happiness as is good for any of the children of Adam.
———R. H. TAWNEY

*W*hat a wonderful life I've had! I only wish I'd realized it sooner.
———COLETTE

*H*appiness is not a state to arrive at, but a manner of traveling.
———MARGARET LEE RUNBECK

It is the chiefest point of happiness that a man
is willing to be what he is.
———Erasmus

Joy is not in things; it is in us.
———Richard Wagner

Whoever is happy will make others happy too.
———Anne Frank

Happiness is not best achieved by those who
seek it directly.
———Bertrand Russell

*H*appiness is mostly a by-product of doing what makes us feel fulfilled.

—BENJAMIN SPOCK

*M*ankind has become so much one family that we cannot insure our own prosperity except by insuring that of everyone else. If you wish to be happy yourself, you must resign yourself to seeing others also happy.

—BERTRAND RUSSELL

*I*f only we'd stop trying to be happy, we could have a pretty good time.

—EDITH WHARTON

Happiness is a mystery like religion, and should never be rationalized.
—G. K. Chesterton

There is only one way to happiness and that is to cease worrying about things which are beyond the power of will.
—Epictetus

More and more it seems the faithful distort God's message and hear, "Love thy neighbor, hate thyself."
—Michael Levine

$\mathcal{H}$appiness is equilibrium. Shift your weight. Equilibrium is pragmatic. You have to get everything into proportion. You compensate, rebalance yourself so that you maintain your angle to your world. When the world shifts, you shift.

—Tom Stoppard

$\mathcal{C}$ompare what you want with what you have, and you'll be unhappy; compare what you deserve with what you have, and you'll be happy.

—Evan Esar

*T*alk happiness. The world is sad enough
Without your woe. No path is wholly rough.
— ELLA WHEELER WILCOX

*Y*our best shot at happiness, self-worth, and personal satisfaction—the things that constitute
real success—is not in earning as much as you
can but in performing as well as you can something that you consider worthwhile. Whether
that is healing the sick, giving hope to the
hopeless, adding to the beauty of the world, or
saving the world from nuclear holocaust, I cannot tell you.
— WILLIAM RASPBERRY

*H*appiness is like a cat. If you try to coax it or call it, it will avoid you. It will never come. But if you pay no attention to it and go about your business, you'll find it rubbing against your legs and jumping into your lap. So forget pursuing happiness. Pin your hopes on work, on family, on learning, on knowing, on loving. Forget pursuing happiness, pursue these other things, and with luck happiness will come.

—WILLIAM BENNETT

*N*o matter how dull, or how mean, or how wise a man is, he feels that happiness is his indisputable right.

—HELEN KELLER

*W*e find a delight in the beauty and happiness
of children, that makes the heart too big for
the body.

— RALPH WALDO EMERSON

*S*care not much for gold or land;—
    Give me a mortgage here and there,—
Some good bank-stock, some note of hand,
    Or trifling railroad share,—
I only ask that Fortune send
A *little* more than I shall spend.

— OLIVER WENDELL HOLMES SR.

What wisdom, what warning can prevail against gladness? There is no law so strong which a little gladness may not transgress.
—HENRY DAVID THOREAU

Grief can take care of itself, but to get the full value of a joy you must have somebody to divide it with.
—MARK TWAIN

Derive happiness in oneself from a good day's work, from illuminating the fog that surrounds us.
—HENRI MATISSE

*H*appiness must be cultivated. It is like
character. It is not a thing to be safely let
alone for a moment, or it will run to weeds.
— ELIZABETH STUART PHELPS

*T*he U.S. Constitution doesn't guarantee
happiness, only the pursuit of it. You have
to catch up to it yourself.
— BENJAMIN FRANKLIN

*I*n the pursuit of happiness, the difficulty lies
in knowing when you have caught up.
— R. H. GRENVILLE

You have to sniff out joy, keep your nose to the
joy-trail.

—BUFFY SAINTE-MARIE

It is not easy to find happiness in ourselves, and it
is impossible to find it elsewhere.

—AGNES REPPLIER

The happiest people seem to be those who have no
particular reason for being happy except that
they are so.

—DEAN WILLIAM R. INGE

The best way to secure future happiness is to be as happy as is rightfully possible to-day.
— CHARLES W. ELIOT

Anyone who thinks money will make you happy doesn't have money. Happiness is more difficult to obtain than money.
— DAVID GEFFEN

It is neither wealth nor splendor, but tranquility and occupation, which give happiness.
— THOMAS JEFFERSON

*H*appiness to me is wine,
Effervescent, superfine.
Full of tang and fiery pleasure.
— AMY LOWELL

*H*appiness sneaks in through a door you didn't
know you left open.
— JOHN BARRYMORE

I used to think it was great to disregard happiness, to press on to a high goal, careless,
disdainful of it. But now I see that there is
nothing so great as to be capable of happiness.
— ANNE GILCHRIST

*I*f you want to be happy, be.
⟶ LEO TOLSTOY

*O*ne joy scatters a hundred griefs.
⟶ CHINESE PROVERB

*O*ne is happy as a result of one's own efforts, once
one knows the necessary ingredients of happiness—simple tastes, a certain degree of
courage, self-denial to a point, love of work,
and, above all, a clear conscience. Happiness is
no vague dream, of that I now feel certain.
⟶ GEORGE SAND

*E*very time I talk to a savant I feel quite sure that
happiness is no longer a possibility. Yet when I
talk with my gardener, I'm convinced of the
opposite.

———BERTRAND RUSSELL

*T*here is that in me—I do not know what it is—
but I know it is in me. . . .
I do not know it—it is without name—it is a word
unsaid,
It is not in any dictionary, utterance, symbol. . . .
Do you see O my brothers and sisters?
It is not chaos or death—it is form, union, plan—it
is eternal life—it is Happiness.

———WALT WHITMAN

The grand essentials of happiness are: something
to do, something to love, and something to
hope for.

—ALLAN K. CHALMERS

The happiness which we receive from ourselves is
greater than that which we obtain from our
surroundings. . . . The world in which a man
lives shapes itself chiefly by the way in which
he looks at it.

—ARTHUR SCHOPENHAUER

Happiness is a change of trouble.

—MALVINA HOFFMAN

$\mathcal{T}$he art of being happy lies in the power of
extracting happiness from common things.
—HENRY WARD BEECHER

$\mathcal{W}$ork and live to serve others, to leave the world
a little better than you found it, and garner for
yourself as much peace of mind as you can.
This is happiness.
—DAVID SARNOFF

$\mathcal{S}$o long as we can lose some happiness,
we possess some.
—BOOTH TARKINGTON

*W*hen, a small child, . . . I thought that success spelled happiness. I was wrong. Happiness is like a butterfly which appears and delights us for one brief moment, but soon flits away.
——ANNA PAVLOVA

*G*etting what you go after is success; but liking it while you are getting it is happiness.
——BERTHA DAMON

*M*ost people ask for happiness on condition. Happiness can only be felt if you don't set any conditions.
——ARTUR RUBENSTEIN

A string of excited, fugitive, miscellaneous
pleasures is not happiness; happiness resides
in imaginative reflection and judgment, when
the *picture* of one's life, or of human life, as it
truly has been or is, satisfies the will, and is
gladly accepted.
—GEORGE SANTAYANA

*T*he greatest happiness you can have is knowing
that you do not necessarily require happiness.
—WILLIAM SAROYAN

*H*appiness comes in the full employment of our faculties in some pursuit.

—HARRIET MARTINEAU

A happy life must be to a great extent a quiet life, for it is only in an atmosphere of quiet that true joy can live.

—BERTRAND RUSSELL

A great obstacle to happiness is to expect too much happiness.

—BERNARD FONTENELLE

*W*hat right have we to happiness?
—HENRIK IBSEN

*H*appiness and Beauty are by-products.
—GEORGE BERNARD SHAW

*H*appiness is not something you get, but something you do.
—MARCELENE COX

*H*appiness is that state of consciousness which proceeds from the achievement of one's values.
—AYN RAND

Happiness is not a possession to be prized, it is a
quality of thought, a state of mind.
—DAPHNE DU MAURIER

Happiness is excitement that has found a settling
down place, but there is always a little corner
that keeps floating around.
—E. L. KONIGSBURG

No one has the right to consume happiness without producing it.
—HELEN KELLER

One of the great hindrances to happiness in the present day is our tendency to standardize our conception of it.
— J. E. BUCKROSE

Life may take away happiness. But it can't take away having had it.
— ELLEN GLASGOW

Happiness is not a matter of events; it depends upon the tides of the mind.
— ALICE MEYNELL

*W*here your pleasure is, there is your treasure:
where your treasure is, there your heart; where
your heart, there your happiness.
— SAINT AUGUSTINE

*T*he unendurable is the beginning of the curve
of joy.
— DJUNA BARNES

*H*appiness is a matter of one's most ordinary
everyday mode of consciousness being busy and
lively and unconcerned with self.
— IRIS MURDOCH

*H*ave your heart right with Christ, and He will
visit you often, and so turn weekdays into
Sundays, meals into sacraments, homes into
temples, and earth into heaven.

—CHARLES HADDON SPURGEON

*I*t is interesting to note that even Jefferson never
proposed happiness as an inalienable right. Our
constitution talks of a right only for the *pursuit*
of happiness. Ours for the seeking and the win-
ning! Not free. Happiness is the result, the
product, of endeavor. Never God-given.
Happiness is only God-*permitted*.

—*PERMANIZED PAPER QUARTERLY*

*S*urely the strange beauty of the world must
somehow rest on pure joy!
—LOUISE BOGAN

*E*ven if happiness forgets you a little bit, never
completely forget about it.
—JACQUES PRÉVERT

*H*appy is the soul that has something to look
backward to with pride, and something to
look forward to with hope.
—OLIVER G. WILSON

A month after last Christmas, I received an anonymous card in the mail—meaning I have absolutely no idea who sent it to me or why. Because its message describes a unique component of happiness in a way that almost bowled me over with its originality and profundity, I have thus far had over a hundred copies made of it and sent them to my friends. At first reading, no more than one out of ten of my friends have understood it, but the few who did "get it" are extraordinarily wise people.

*On the front of the card there is a colorful picture of a woman dressed in blue sitting over a chessboard. The figure of the woman and other aspects of the painting strongly suggest that she could be the Virgin Mary. Above the painting in large letters is written the single word "*CHECKMATE.*" Below the painting, in smaller letters, the following question is asked: "What is the difference between your experience of Existence and that of a Saint?"*

The answer to that question is provided on the inside

of the card. I immediately recognized by its style that the author was in all probability a member of a group of extraordinarily wise Muslim mystics or Sufis who flourished in thirteenth-century Persia. Indeed, the message was credited to one of the more famous of those men, known as Hafiz. Hafiz's answer to the above posed question was:

The saint knows
That the spiritual path
Is a sublime chess game with God
And that the Beloved
Has just made such a Fantastic move
That the saint is now
Continually tripping over with Joy
And bursting with Laughter
And saying, "I surrender."

Whereas, my dear,
I am afraid you still think
You have a thousand serious moves.

THE TEXT OF THIS BOOK IS SET IN GRANJON
BY MSPACE, KATONAH, NEW YORK

BOOK DESIGN BY MAURA FADDEN ROSENTHAL